50 Manager Interview Questions

Curveballs, Model Responses, and Pro Tips to Help You Nail the Interview and Get the Job

Kennedy Williams

ISBN 979-8-9860736-2-0

50 Manager Interview Questions

50 Questions, Model Responses, and Pro Tips to Help
You Nail the Interview and Get the Job

INTRODUCTION

So, you're ready to embark upon the process of interviewing for a managerial position! The interview process can be both exciting and nerve-wracking — it creates an opportunity to showcase your skills, knowledge, and passion for management and leadership, but it can also be intimidating to face a panel to answer their questions on the fly. Of course, that's why it's so important to be well-prepared for your interview and to make the most of the opportunity before you.

This book is here to help you do exactly that. It's a comprehensive guide to the interview process, filled with valuable information to help you succeed. In that sense, it should feel like the ultimate study guide. You'll find that it's brimming with a wide range of managerial interview questions, model responses, and pro tips to help you craft the best possible answers. Regardless of whether you're an experienced manager or just starting out, this book promises to meet you where you are and to give you the strongest possible foundation for your next interview.

Beyond that, this book is about *more* than preparing for just the interview itself; it's also about helping you to think critically about your beliefs, to reflect on your philosophies, and to become the best manager you can be. By reading through the questions and model responses, you'll gain valuable insights into what higher level managers, business owners, and executives are looking for in a candidate. You'll learn how to articulate your managerial philosophy and your vision for your leadership, and you'll have the chance to practice your interview skills and build your confidence. In short, there is no way you won't be a stronger candidate, *and* a stronger manager, by the time you get to the other side of this book.

You'll find that this book is divided into three sections. In the first section, you'll find standard questions that are commonly asked during manager interviews. These questions cover a wide array of topics related to your philosophy, your experience, and your ability to manage employees. The second section contains curveballs — unexpected questions that are often intended to catch candidates off guard, and that may not have a clear "correct" answer. And in the third section, you'll find scenarios — realistic, interactive questions that require you to apply your skills and knowledge to tackle a complex, real-world problem. Each of these sections will provide you with a wealth of information and guidance to help you prepare for your interview, to help you carefully consider your leadership philosophy and practices, and to help you succeed in your career as a manager.

That said, where best to begin? First and foremost, it's important to be ready for the most basic but essential question that you are likely to be asked at the start of any interview. This question is the foundation upon which the rest of the interview will be built, and offers an opportunity for you to introduce yourself, explain your interest in the position, and outline the qualities that make you the most appealing candidate for the job. That question is: "Who are you? Go ahead and start us off by telling us about yourself."

Think of this is an incredible open-ended opportunity to introduce yourself to the interview panel, and to give them a sense of who you are. Wield this power to your advantage, and come prepared to impress the group from the onset! It's important not to be long winded, but simultaneously, to provide enough information to make a positive impression. You might want to mention your education, your experience, and any of the most impressive skills or achievements that you'd like to highlight.

For example, you might begin by saying something like: "My name is John Jones, and I am a recent graduate of XYZ University. I received my bachelor's degree in business administration, and I've been working in sales for the past year. Six months ago, I was promoted to a team leadership position, and I've had a lot of success helping to organize, motivate, and lead my colleagues. The managerial responsibilities I've taken on have been really rewarding, and I'm eager to step into a position that allows me to do more of that work. I'm very excited about the opportunity to talk with you today, and I can't wait to make a positive contribution to the company."

A common follow-up question you are very likely to be asked is, "Why this position? Why our company?" As with the previous question, this is your opportunity to explain why you are interested in the specific job you've applied to, as well as the specific organization or business; come prepared to make a specific case as to why you're a great fit. The strongest responses always come from candidates who have done their research, that are specific about what attracted them to the position, and that can speak to the specific qualities they can contribute to that particular job. Conversely, candidates that offer overly general responses, or responses that don't showcase their passion for a particular position (i.e. "I was hoping for a general management position, but I figured I'd apply to this leadership role just because..."), are immediately at a disadvantage. A little research goes a long way, and can help to make you stand out as a candidate from the very start of the interview — so do your homework! Review the business or company website, peruse the most recent news or social media postings, and check out any additional information about current initiatives that you might be able to get your hands on.

You might say something like: "I am excited about the opportunity to join your team at ABC Company because I believe that your commitment to transform the way people access their bank funds completely aligns with my own philosophy about the future of financial technology. I also noticed that one of the initiatives promoted by the company is to promote more diversity, which is something I have experience in, am passionate about, and am eager to contribute to. My own experiences and background will definitely enable me to make a unique contribution to the company on this front, and likewise, I know that I want to work for a company that shares my values. I think it's a great fit for both of us."

The third foundational question that you're likely to be asked is a doozy — one that you've surely thought about and perhaps even written about in management preparation courses. And, frankly, this question is probably too broad to answer comprehensively in a single sitting. The question is, "What is your management style?" As with the previous two questions, consider this an open-ended opportunity to highlight your most impressive attributes: outline your beliefs about management, explain how you approach your work as a leader, and wherever possible, connect these ideas to your previous responses, i.e. how this aligns with the specific position and the organization.

As always, it's important to be clear and concise, and to provide concrete examples to illustrate your points.

Here, you might say something like: "My management style is a combination of several different approaches. I believe in leading by example and setting a strong vision for the team to follow. I also place a strong emphasis on clear communication and transparency in order to ensure that everyone is on the same page and working towards the same goals. In terms of decision-making, I believe in being collaborative and involving my team members in the process as much as possible. I also believe in being flexible and adaptable, and I am always open to new ideas and perspectives. Additionally, I believe in fostering a positive and supportive work environment, where team members feel valued, have the autonomy to take ownership of their work, and have the support they need to be successful."

Once you've taken the time to think about these important foundational questions and feel prepared to talk about your answers in an interview, you can move on to the rest of this book with confidence.

To get the most out of this resource as you prepare for your interview, review the questions and model responses carefully and think about how you would answer them yourself — in your voice, infused with your ideas, and true to your beliefs. As you read through the questions, take note of any that you are unsure about or that you feel you might need to practice more extensively. Then, use the model responses as a guide to craft your own personal responses that feel comfortable, conversational, authentic, and true to you.

One effective way to practice your answers is to have friends or family members pose the questions to you in a mock interview format. This might feel silly at first, but it can definitely help you to get a feel for the flow of the conversation and to practice answering the questions under simulated interview conditions. You might even try interviewing yourself by voice-recording the questions and playing them back, one at a time, after you speak your answer aloud. As you practice, pay attention to your body language, your tone of voice, and your overall presentation. Try to be as natural and authentic as possible, and don't be afraid to ask for feedback.

In addition to reviewing the questions and practicing your answers, be sure not to overlook general professional interview etiquette. This includes dressing appropriately (in business attire), speaking respectfully and formally, and being punctual. You may also want to consider creating a portfolio of your work to bring to the interview. (This isn't essential, but it rarely hurts.)

Overall, the key to success in a managerial interview is preparation. By reviewing the questions and model responses in this book, practicing your answers, and paying attention to professional etiquette, you can increase your confidence and make a strong impression on the interview panel. The effort you put in beforehand will surely help to set you apart during the interview process, and will pay off in the end! Remember, the interview is your chance to showcase your skills and passion for management and leadership, and with the right preparation, you can succeed and land the position you want.

Be yourself, stay positive, and good luck on your search!

STANDARD QUESTIONS

Question 1
How do you envision yourself leading a team and achieving success?

Model Response

As a manager, I envision myself leading my team using clear communication, collaboration, and a focus on individual and collective goals. I believe that effective leadership involves setting clear expectations and goals for the team, as well as providing ongoing support and resources to help team members achieve success.

To create a successful and cohesive team, I believe it is important to establish a foundation built on respect, that promotes open lines of communication, and that encourages open and honest feedback. This includes regularly scheduled team meetings, as well as being available to team members for one-on-one discussions when needed. By fostering an open and inclusive working environment, team members generally feel more comfortable sharing ideas and concerns, which can ultimately lead to better decision-making and problem-solving.

I also believe that it is important to focus on the strengths and development of individual team members. By providing ongoing training and support, and by regularly giving constructive feedback, I can help team members grow and develop their skills. This not only benefits the team as a whole, but also helps team members feel more fulfilled and engaged in their work.

As a manager, I see myself as a facilitator, rather than a dictatorial leader. I believe that it is important to empower team members to make decisions and take ownership of their work, while also being available to provide guidance and support when needed. By fostering an environment of trust and collaboration, I believe that my team can achieve great things together.

Pro Tips

- Be specific and provide concrete examples of your leadership style and approach. This will help the interviewer get a better understanding of how you envision yourself leading a team.
- Emphasize the importance of open communication, collaboration, and individual and team development.
- To the greatest extent possible, demonstrate how you are adaptable and able to adjust your leadership style to fit the needs of different team members and situations.

Question 2
Can you provide an example of a time when you effectively managed a challenging situation or conflict within a team?

Model Response

A time when I effectively managed a challenging situation within a team was when a project was at risk of falling behind schedule due to several team members experiencing unexpected personal and professional challenges. As the project manager, it was my responsibility to find a way to keep the project on track while also supporting and accommodating the needs of my team members.

I approached the situation by first taking the time to understand the specific challenges that each team member was facing. This involved having one-on-one conversations with each team member to assess their needs and concerns. I then worked with the team to come up with a plan that would allow us to meet our project deadlines while also providing the necessary support and accommodations for team members who were experiencing challenges.

One key aspect of this plan was to reassign certain tasks and responsibilities within the team to better utilize the strengths and capabilities of each team member. This allowed us to continue making progress on the project while also ensuring that each team member was able to manage their workload effectively given their personal and professional commitments.

In addition to reassigning tasks and responsibilities, I also implemented regular check-ins with each team member to ensure that they had the support they needed to stay on track with their work. This included providing additional resources and support as needed, as well as being available to discuss any issues or concerns that arose.

Ultimately, through clear communication, collaboration, and a focus on the needs of individual team members, we were able to successfully complete the project on time and to the satisfaction of our clients.

Pro Tips

- Provide specific examples of your approach to managing challenging situations or conflicts. Demonstrate your understanding of your problem-solving skills, your ability to handle difficult situations, and your ability to adapt to changing circumstances.
- Emphasize the importance of clear communication, collaboration, and a focus on the needs of individual team members in your approach to managing challenging situations.
- Show how you're able to come up with creative solutions to address the challenges faced by your team and how those solutions ultimately resulted in a successful outcome.

Question 3
How do you approach setting and achieving goals for both yourself and your team?

Model Response

Setting and achieving goals is crucial for both personal and team success. To approach goal setting, I like to follow a structured process that includes defining the goal, breaking it down into smaller, achievable tasks, and regularly tracking progress.

To set goals for both myself and my team, I think it's imperative to first take the time to understand the overall strategy and objectives of the organization. This helps to ensure that the goals I set for myself and my team are aligned with the larger goals of the company, and that we're all rowing in the same direction.

Once I have a clear understanding of the desired outcomes, I work with my team to define specific, measurable, attainable, relevant, and time-bound (SMART) goals. This involves breaking down the larger goal into smaller, more manageable tasks and setting clear deadlines for completion.

To ensure that we're on track to achieve our goals, I regularly review and assess progress with my team. This includes setting up regular check-ins to track progress and identify any obstacles or challenges that may arise. If necessary, I work with my team to adjust our approach or realign our goals as needed.

To support the achievement of our goals, I also provide my team with the necessary resources and support. This includes providing ongoing training and development opportunities, as well as being available to discuss any issues or concerns that may arise.

Pro Tips

- Be specific and provide concrete examples of how you have set and achieved goals for yourself and your team in the past. This can convey a clearer understanding of your approach to goal setting and achievement.

- Emphasize the importance of using a structured process, such as the SMART goal framework, to set and achieve goals. If you aren't familiar with a goal setting framework yet, consider doing some research and perhaps even setting a personal SMART goal prior to the interview.

- Show how you are able to adapt and adjust your approach to goal setting and achievement as needed, based on the needs and circumstances of your team and of the larger organization.

Question 4
How do you ensure that team members are engaged and motivated in their work?

Model Response

As a manager, I believe that ensuring that team members are engaged and motivated in their work is crucial for team success. To do this, I focus on creating a positive and inclusive team culture, providing ongoing support and development opportunities, and setting clear expectations and goals for the team.

One key aspect of ensuring team engagement and motivation is fostering a positive and inclusive team culture. This involves creating an environment where team members feel valued, heard, and supported. I do this by regularly soliciting feedback from team members, actively listening to their concerns and ideas, and providing ongoing support and resources to help them succeed. Ensuring that all team members have an understanding of the organization's larger vision, mission, and goals is another important part of fostering buy-in, motivation, and meaningful engagement.

To support the professional development of my team members, I believe in providing ongoing training and development opportunities wherever possible and appropriate. This might include in-house training, as well as external workshops or conferences. Investing in the development of the team can go a long way.

In addition to fostering a positive team culture and providing development opportunities, I also believe it is important to set clear expectations and goals for the team. This includes setting specific and measurable goals, and regularly reviewing and tracking progress towards these goals. By setting clear expectations and goals, team members can see the impact of their work and feel more motivated to contribute to the success of the team.

Pro Tips

- Be prepared to share specific examples of how you foster a positive and inclusive team culture. This could include examples from the past, or hypothetical practices that you are looking forward to implementing in the future.
- Emphasize the importance of investing in all members of the team and the organization through ongoing support and development opportunities.
- Show how you have set and tracked clear goals for yourself, and if possible, for your team, to promote motivation and engagement.

Question 5
How do you prioritize tasks and delegate responsibilities within a team?

Model Response
As a manager, I believe that effective task prioritization and delegation is crucial for ensuring that the team is able to work efficiently and effectively. To approach task prioritization and delegation, I follow a structured process that involves defining the task, assessing the skills and capabilities of team members, and regularly reviewing and adjusting as needed.

To prioritize tasks, I first take the time to understand the overall goals and objectives of the team and the organization. This helps me to identify which tasks are most important and need to be completed first. I then use a variety of tools and techniques, such as a task matrix or a prioritization matrix, to assess the relative importance and urgency of each task.

Once I have identified and prioritized the tasks, I assess the skills and capabilities of my team members to determine who is best suited to complete each task. This involves taking into account the individual strengths and development needs of each team member, as well as the specific requirements of each task.

To ensure that tasks are completed effectively and efficiently, I regularly review and adjust my approach to task prioritization and delegation as needed. This may involve reassigning tasks or responsibilities based on changing priorities or the evolving needs of the team.

Pro Tips
- Explain how you have prioritized tasks and delegated responsibilities within a team in the past, either as a team leader, or as a team member having

taken a leadership initiative within the group.

- Emphasize the importance of aligning tasks with the overall goals and objectives of the team and the organization, and the necessity to delegate tasks in order to increase efficiency.
- Show how you are able to adapt and adjust your approach to task prioritization and delegation as needed, based on the changing needs and circumstances of the team.

Question 6
How do you approach giving feedback to team members?

Model Response

Providing ongoing feedback to team members is crucial for their professional development and for the overall success of the team. To approach this, I make it a point to offer specific, timely, and constructive feedback on a regular basis, and wherever appropriate, solicit feedback from team members or members of the organization to inform that feedback.

To make sure that the feedback I'm providing is effective, I believe it's important to be specific and to provide concrete examples — whether the feedback is positive or constructive. This helps to clarify for team members what they are doing well and where they can improve. I also try to provide feedback in a timely manner, so that team members can address any issues or concerns while they are still relevant and actionable, when it matters most.

In addition to providing specific and timely feedback, I also try to focus on the constructive aspect of feedback, rather than just pointing out problems or mistakes. I do this by providing specific suggestions for how team members can improve and by offering support and resources to help them achieve their goals.

I also regularly solicit feedback from team members by setting up regular check-ins or asking for feedback on specific tasks or projects. By regularly soliciting feedback, I'm able to get a better understanding of how team members are feeling and what they need to be successful.

Pro Tips
- Be specific and provide concrete examples of how you have provided both positive and constructive

feedback to team members in the past. This is a great opportunity for you to illustrate your approach to feedback.

- Emphasize the importance of being timely and providing constructive feedback, rather than just pointing out problems or mistakes. Likewise, emphasize the importance of confronting problematic issues as they arise.
- Show how you regularly solicit feedback from team members to ensure that you are providing ongoing support and development. This can also demonstrate that you value feedback yourself, and how you consider meaningful feedback to be a two-way street.

Question 7
How do you foster a positive and inclusive team culture?

Model Response

Fostering a positive and inclusive team culture is crucial for the overall success and productivity of any team. To approach fostering a positive and inclusive team culture, I focus on building strong relationships with team members, promoting open communication and collaboration, and creating a supportive and respectful work environment.

To build strong relationships with team members, I believe it is important to regularly engage with them and show an interest in their professional and personal lives. This may involve setting up regular one-on-one meetings or social activities outside of work. By building strong relationships with team members, I am able to create a more trusting and supportive environment where team members feel comfortable sharing ideas and concerns.

To promote open communication and collaboration, I encourage team members to share their ideas and opinions, and to actively listen to the ideas and concerns of others. I also make sure to provide opportunities for team members to work together and collaborate on projects. By fostering open communication and collaboration, I believe that team members will feel more engaged and motivated in their work.

I also make it a point to clearly communicate the values and expectations of the team and the organization. I encourage team members to respect the diversity and differences of their colleagues and to create an inclusive and welcoming environment for each other. Fostering a positive culture is a team effort, and is critical to ensure that everyone feels valued, motivated, and ready to contribute to the success of the team.

Pro Tips

- Be prepared to share specific strategies that you might use to promote a positive culture, or examples of how you've built strong relationships with team members in the past.
- Emphasize the importance of promoting open communication and collaboration within the team.
- Show how you've created a supportive and respectful work environment for team members, along with how this has contributed to the overall success of the team.

Question 8
How do you handle team members who are not meeting their performance expectations?

Model Response

As a manager, it is my responsibility to ensure that team members are meeting their performance expectations. When I encounter a team member who is not meeting their performance expectations, I take the necessary steps of identifying the root cause of the issue, setting clear goals and expectations to address that issue, and providing ongoing support and resources to help the team member improve.

To identify the root cause, I would first take time to understand the specific challenges and needs of the team member. This would involve having one-on-one conversations with that person to assess their concerns and goals, and also seeking feedback from other team members or supervisors. By getting to the root cause, I'd be much better able to identify solutions and to provide the necessary support and resources.

Once I've identified the root cause of the issue, I would work with the team member to set clear goals and expectations for their performance. This involves setting specific, measurable, attainable, relevant, and time-bound (SMART) goals and regularly reviewing and tracking progress towards these goals. By setting clear goals and expectations, team members are able to understand what is expected of them and how they can improve.

To provide ongoing support and resources, I would make sure that the team member has access to the necessary training and development opportunities, as well as any other resources or support they might need to improve their performance. I would also regularly check in with the team member to provide ongoing feedback and support, and to ensure that they stay on track to meet their performance goals.

Pro Tips

- Offer examples of how you have addressed team members who were not meeting their performance expectations in the past. Strive to give the interviewer a better understanding of your approach to addressing performance issues.
- Emphasize the importance of identifying the root cause of the issue and setting clear goals and expectations in addressing performance issues.
- Elaborate on how you provide ongoing support and resources to help team members improve their performance.

Question 9

How do you adapt your leadership style to fit the needs and personalities of different team members?

Model Response

All people are different, so adapting one's leadership style to fit the needs and personalities of different team members can be crucial for the overall success and productivity of the team. To approach adapting my leadership style, I focus on building strong relationships with team members, regularly soliciting feedback, and being open to new approaches and ideas.

To build strong relationships with team members, I believe it is important to regularly engage with them and show an interest in their professional and personal lives. This can happen organically through one-on-one meetings or social activities outside of work, and by building these relationships, I'd be much better able to get an understanding of everybody's individual needs and personalities. This, of course, would be key to knowing how to adapt my leadership style accordingly.

To regularly solicit feedback from team members, I would set up regular check-ins or ask for feedback on specific tasks or projects. In doing so, I would be able to get a better understanding of how team members are feeling and what they might need in order to be successful. These insights would help me to adapt my leadership style to better meet the needs of the team.

In addition to building strong relationships and regularly soliciting feedback, I also believe it is important to be open to new approaches and ideas. To that end, I am always open to feedback and suggestions from team members, and I'm willing to try new approaches or methods if they are likely to be more effective. By being open to new ideas, I'm able to better adapt my leadership style to fit the needs and personalities of different team members.

Pro Tips

- Share examples that showcase how you've adapted your leadership style to fit the needs and personalities of different team members in the past.
- Emphasize the importance of building strong relationships with team members and regularly soliciting feedback in order to better understand their needs and personalities.
- Demonstrate that you are open to new approaches and ideas, and that you are willing to try new methods if they are likely to be beneficial the team.

Question 10

How do you stay up-to-date on industry trends and changes, and how do you incorporate this knowledge into your team's work?

Model Response

For any manager, and for anyone in a leadership position, it's important to stay up-to-date on industry trends and changes in order to ensure that the organization and the team are able to adapt, to stay competitive, and to be as effective as possible. To that end, I regularly research and strive to learn about new developments, and I'm always seeking out opportunities to network with industry experts.

To regularly research and learn about new developments in my industry, I make use of a variety of resources, such as industry publications, online articles, blogs, and professional development workshops and conferences. I also make an effort to stay informed about changes in regulations or policies that may impact the work of my team.

As far as networking with industry experts to learn from their experiences, I like to attend industry events and join related professional organizations and groups. By networking with industry experts, I'm able to stay up-to-date on the latest trends and best practices in my field.

To incorporate this knowledge into the work of my team, I make sure to regularly communicate new developments and trends to team members and encourage them to stay informed as well. I also encourage team members to share their own insights and ideas about how to incorporate new knowledge and trends into our work.

Pro Tips

- Provide specific examples of how you have stayed up-to-date on industry trends and changes in the past. Be prepared to name specific organizations, workshops, blogs, or other resources that you might use for this purpose.
- Emphasize the importance of regularly researching and learning about new developments in your industry, as well as seeking out opportunities to network with industry experts.
- Elaborate on how you put new learning to work by regularly communicating new developments and trends to your team.

Question 11

How do you build and maintain strong relationships with stakeholders, both within and outside of the organization?

Model Response

To approach building and maintaining strong relationships with stakeholders both within and outside of the organization, I focus on regular communication, collaboration, and transparency.

Where regular communication is concerned, I believe that it's important to keep stakeholders continuously informed about the work of the team, as appropriate for those stakeholders' interests, and any developments or changes that might impact them. This could involve setting up regular meetings with stakeholder groups, but more likely would be accomplished using email or other communication tools to stay in touch. By prioritizing regular communication with stakeholders, I would build trust and understanding, and I would be better able to ensure that their concerns and needs are being addressed.

As far as fostering collaboration, I would encourage team members to actively seek out opportunities to work with stakeholders to whatever extent might be appropriate, and likewise for involving stakeholders in different stages of the decision-making process. This might involve inviting stakeholders to contribute their ideas and opinions during meetings or workshops, or asking for their input on specific projects or initiatives. By promoting collaboration with stakeholders in this fashion, we would inevitable achieve better outcomes and build stronger relationships.

In terms of being transparent with stakeholders, I believe it is important to be open and honest about the work of the team and any challenges or issues that may arise. This involves being open to feedback and questions from stakeholders, and being proactive in addressing any concerns or issues that may arise. Transparency with stakeholders is crucial for building trust, and for creating more open and collaborative relationships.

Pro Tips

- If possible, share examples of how you have built and maintained strong relationships with stakeholders in the past. If not, share specific examples of how you might do this in the future. Focus on explaining your approach to building and maintaining relationships.
- Emphasize the importance of regular communication, collaboration, and transparency in building and maintaining strong relationships with stakeholders.
- Share any tools or techniques that you've used in the past to build and maintain strong relationships with stakeholders, such as regular meetings or check-ins, email or other communication tools, or workshops or focus groups.

Question 12
How do you handle difficult conversations with team members, such as addressing performance issues or addressing conflicts?

Model Response

Handling difficult conversations with team members in a constructive and respectful manner is crucial. To accomplish this, I often like to focus on clear goals or expectations that have been set and that can be referenced during the conversation. The more objective I can make the conversation, in terms of what performance issues or conflicts might exist, the easier that difficult conversation becomes. Wherever possible, I also like to focus on plans for moving forward in a positive and proactive way, so that the difficult conversation can have a beneficial outcome for both the team member and the work we're doing in the company.

In preparing for a difficult conversation, I think it's important to set clear goals for the meeting, and to do so, I make sure to identify the specific issues or concerns that need to be addressed and the corresponding desired outcomes of the conversation. This ensures that we are able to make progress towards resolving the issue. I also make sure to gather any relevant information or evidence that may be needed to support my points or address any concerns.

I'll also add that an effective way to approach a difficult conversations is often to focus on being clear and respectful. The basic principles of good communication are more important than ever. Part of that means encouraging team members to share their own ideas and opinions, and actively listening to their concerns. Doing so can help pave the way to finding more effective and mutually beneficial solutions to difficult issues.

Pro Tips

- If you have handled difficult conversations with team members in the past, be prepared to share these examples.
- Emphasize the importance of setting clear goals and preparing in advance for difficult conversations, with the overall intention of making progress on the problem at hand.
- Show how you are open to feedback and suggestions during difficult conversations and consider the needs and perspectives of team members. This can provide a means for you to speak to how creative, unexpected, and mutually beneficial solutions might be uncovered.

Question 13
How do you support the professional development of your team members?

Model Response

I believe that supporting the professional development of team members is crucial for the overall success and productivity of the team, and the organization. To approach this, I would focus on setting clear goals for the team and for individual team members, before seeking out and providing opportunities for learning and development in these areas.

To set clear goals for the professional development of team members, I would work with them to identify current gaps in their knowledge, skills they might need to improve on to offer greater value to the team, and perhaps even their career aspirations along with the skills and experiences they need to achieve them. By using this context to set clear goals, I would be able to help team members focus their efforts in a meaningful way.

To provide opportunities for learning and development, I would encourage team members to take advantage of internal or external training and development programs, as well as seek out learning opportunities on their own. I would also encourage team members to seek out new challenges and responsibilities that will help them to develop new skills and experiences. Additionally, by tracking their progress, we might measure the impact of these learning experiences on the value that these individuals bring to the team.

Pro Tips
- Help the interviewer get a better understanding of your approach to supporting professional

development by sharing specific examples of how you have supported the professional development of team members in the past, as well as how you have treated your own professional development.

- Emphasize the importance of setting and pursuing clear goals, as well as your role in providing opportunities for learning and development to support your team members.
- Show how you regularly solicit feedback from team members and use this information to identify areas where they may need additional support or development.

Question 14
How do you encourage innovation and creativity within your team?

Model Response

Encouraging innovation and creativity within my team is important for driving new ideas and approaches, and for staying competitive in our industry. To encourage innovation and creativity, I would focus on creating an open and collaborative culture, providing opportunities for exploration and experimentation, and regularly soliciting feedback.

When it comes to creating an open and collaborative culture, I would encourage team members to share their ideas and opinions, and to actively listen to the ideas of others. By fostering this kind of a safe and open environment, team members are more likely to offer creative ideas and to take risks in a low-stakes space. I would also encourage team members to seek out opportunities to collaborate with others, both within and outside of the team.

To provide opportunities for exploration and experimentation, I would also encourage team members to try out new approaches and techniques and to take risks in their work. They would also be encouraged to seek out new learning opportunities and to explore new technologies or methods that may be relevant to their work. By providing these kind of open-ended opportunities for exploration and experimentation, I believe that team members would be primed to come up with innovative ideas.

To regularly solicit feedback from team members, I would set up regular check-ins or ask for feedback on specific tasks or projects. I might also include this as a standing item for regularly scheduled meetings to better incorporate the process of soliciting feedback into our culture. This would help everyone to feel more comfortable questioning the status quo, raising concerns about problems or workflows that could be made more efficient, and collaboratively uncovering resources to help us all become more innovative and creative.

Pro Tips

- Demonstrate how you have encouraged innovation and creativity within your team in the past, or how you would scale personal practices that you implement to foster innovation and creativity to your entire team.
- Emphasize the importance of creating an open and collaborative culture and providing opportunities for exploration and experimentation in encouraging innovation and creativity within your team.
- Demonstrate how you would regularly solicit feedback from team members and use that information to identify areas where they might need additional support or resources to be more innovative and creative.

Question 15
How do you handle competing priorities and time management as a manager?

Model Response

As a manager, handling competing priorities and time management can be a challenge, especially in fast-paced or high-stress environments. To approach handling competing priorities and time management, I focus on goal setting, task prioritization, and being open to feedback and suggestions.

To set clear goals for my work as a manager, I make sure to identify the most important tasks and priorities for the team and for myself, and work with team members to set specific targets and deadlines. This helps to focus all of our efforts, and it ensures that we are able to make progress towards achieving our goals.

To prioritize tasks, I use a variety of tools and techniques, such as creating to-do lists, using time-management apps and software, and even the simple process of breaking larger tasks into smaller, more manageable chunks. I also regularly review my priorities and adjust my schedule as needed to ensure that I'm able to focus on the most important tasks first.

As far as being open to feedback and suggestions, I also believe that it's important to encourage team members to share their ideas about how our goals might be approached more efficiently.

Pro Tips
- Be specific about how you have handled competing priorities and time management in a leadership role in the past. If you have specific tools that you can speak to, such as digital calendar software, time-triggered notifications, or collaborative project management software, you might want to share

them with the interviewer.

- Emphasize the importance of being purposeful when setting clear goals and prioritizing tasks in order to handle competing priorities and time management.
- Show how you are open to feedback and suggestions from team members when looking to enhance efficiency and to manage competing priorities in an effective manner.

Question 16
How do you manage projects and ensure they are completed on time and within budget?

Model Response

As a manager, managing projects and ensuring that they are completed on time and within budget is a crucial part of my role. To approach project management, I focus on setting clear goals, establishing a project plan, and regularly reviewing progress.

To set clear goals for a project, I make sure to identify the specific objectives and outcomes that we are trying to achieve, as well as the resources and timelines that are needed to complete the project. This is important for focusing our efforts and ensuring that we are able to make progress towards achieving our goals.

To establish a project plan, I work with team members to break the project down into smaller, more manageable tasks and assign responsibilities and deadlines for each task. I also make sure to identify any potential risks or issues that may arise and develop contingency plans to address them. This helps to ensure that the project is completed efficiently and effectively.

And finally, to regularly review progress on a project, I set up regular check-ins or progress meetings with team members to review our progress and address any issues or concerns that may arise. It's essential to continuously track our progress against the project plan and adjust our approach as needed in order to ensure that the project stays on track and is completed on time and within budget.

Pro Tips
- Offer specific and multi-part plan to demonstrate your understanding of how to manage projects and

ensure that they are completed on time. If possible, refer to concrete examples from the past that highlight your experience.

- Emphasize the importance of setting clear goals and establishing a project plan in managing projects and ensuring they are completed on time and within budget.
- Show how you regularly review progress on a project and adjust your approach as needed to stay on track.

Question 17
How do you assess and address any risks or challenges that may arise during a project?

Model Response
As a manager, assessing and addressing risks and challenges that may arise during a project is a central part of the job, so when it comes to risk management, I like to focus on identifying potential risks or challenges early on, before they even arise, so that we can develop contingency plans as we regularly review our progress along the way.

To identify potential risks or challenges early on in a project, I make sure to thoroughly review project plans and consider any potential issues or risks that may arise. That typically involves seeking input from team members or stakeholders, as well as conducting a risk assessment to identify potential pitfalls or challenges. By identifying potential risks or challenges early on, I'm much better able to take proactive steps to address them and prevent them before anything becomes a major issues.

To develop contingency plans that address potential risks and challenges, I think it's important to work collaboratively with the whole team in order to identify alternative approaches or solutions that may be used if an issue arises. It's also important to consider the potential impact of different risks or challenges and prioritize the contingency plans accordingly. At the end of the day, those contingency plans ensure that we are prepared to respond to any issues that may arise and are able to continue making progress towards our goals.

Pro Tips
- Be prepared to provide concrete examples of how you have proactively assessed and addressed risks

or challenges that have arisen during a project in the past.

- Emphasize the importance of identifying potential risks or challenges early on in a project and developing contingency plans to address them. Focus on the benefits of being proactive rather than solely reactive.
- Explain how and why you like to regularly review progress on a project so that you can adjust your approach as needed to stay on track.

Question 18
How do you handle sensitive or confidential information within your team?

Model Response

As a manager, appropriately handling sensitive or confidential information a non-negotiable part of the job. This is true for myself, and for any members of the team that have access to sensitive information. To make sure this is done appropriately and in compliance with any regulations, I focus on clarifying all relevant information handling guidelines and expectations for myself and my team members, training team members on handling sensitive information wherever appropriate, and regularly reviewing our policies and procedures to ensure everything is up-to-date.

To set clear guidelines and expectations for handling sensitive or confidential information within my team, I would make sure to clearly and regularly communicate the importance of confidentiality, and the specific rules and protocols that must be followed when handling sensitive information. This would involve establishing guidelines for sharing or storing sensitive information, as well as setting up specific protocols for handling sensitive information during meetings or discussions.

I would also make sure to provide training or resources that explain the importance of confidentiality and the specific rules and protocols that must be followed to any members of the team for which that training would apply. And, I would also make sure to regularly review these guidelines and expectations myself to ensure that they are understood, followed, and appropriately implemented.

In terms of regularly review our policies and procedures for handling sensitive or confidential information, I would set up regular reviews or audits to ensure that our policies and procedures are up-to-date and effective.

Pro Tips

- If possible, offer examples of how you have handled sensitive or confidential information in the past. If you are unable to provide specific examples, be prepared to showcase your understanding of information handling guidelines that are pertinent to the organization or position. This might include human resources related resources, medical information, or sensitive intellectual property information.

- Emphasize the importance of setting clear guidelines and expectations, and of training team members on handling sensitive or confidential information.

- Show how you regularly review your policies and procedures for handling sensitive or confidential information in order to ensure that they are up-to-date and effective.

Question 19
How do you work with team members who have different working styles or approaches?

Model Response
As a manager, working with team members who have different working styles or approaches can be a challenge, but I believe that it is also an opportunity to learn, to grow, and to better connect with individual members of the team. To that end, I would be open to different perspectives, encourage collaboration across the team, and provide support and resources for different team members as needed, within reason.

I would make sure to listen actively and seek input from team members, even if their perspectives or approaches differ from my own. I would also make sure to consider the needs and perspectives of team members when making decisions or setting goals. By being open to different perspectives, I believe that we would able to find more effective and mutually beneficial solutions to challenges and opportunities.

Regular team meetings or check-ins are also a great way to provide opportunities for team members to share their ideas and work together towards common goals. This would further help me to understand and address different working styles, and to foster a positive and inclusive team culture that values diversity. I believe that we would be able to leverage the strengths and expertise of each team member to achieve our goals.

To provide support and resources as needed, I would be sure to identify the specific needs and goals of individual team members and provide resources or support as needed to help them achieve those goals. This may involve providing training or professional development opportunities, or simply offering guidance or support as needed.

Pro Tips

- Explain how you have effectively worked with team members who have different working styles or approaches in the past. Wherever possible, demonstrate how these differences in working styles were a benefit, not a detriment.
- Emphasize the importance of being open to different perspectives and encouraging collaboration within your team.
- Show how you provide support and resources as needed for individual team members to help them achieve their goals. You might discuss the importance of regularly reviewing the needs and goals of team members to ensure that they have the resources and support they need.

Question 20
How do you handle and resolve conflicts within the team?

Model Response

As a manager, handling and resolving conflicts within the team is probably an understated but incredibly important part of the job. To approach conflict resolution, I try to focus on identifying the root causes of conflicts, facilitating open and honest communication, and working with team members to find mutually beneficial solutions.

To identify the root causes of conflicts within the team, I make sure to listen actively to all team members involved in the conflict and seek to understand their perspectives and concerns. Sometimes, sitting down to mediate a conversation between team members for whom a conflict has arisen can be beneficial. During that conversation, I would make it a point to identify any underlying issues or concerns that might be contributing to the conflict, such as misunderstandings or conflicting goals. By identifying the root causes of conflicts, we would strive to take a more targeted and effective approach to resolving the conflict.

In order to facilitate open and honest communication within the team, I would do my best to consistently create a safe and respectful environment where team members feel comfortable sharing their thoughts and concerns. In these kinds of environments, minor conflicts can be worked out collaboratively before they escalate into more problematic or toxic issues. I would make sure to encourage team members to actively listen to and respect the perspectives of others, and to be open to finding mutually beneficial solutions.

Pro Tips
- Demonstrate your willingness to facilitate or

mediate challenging conversations in a meaningful and respectful way. If possible, offer examples of how you have handled and resolved conflicts within a team in the past.

- Elaborate on the importance of identifying the root causes of conflicts and facilitating open and honest communication within the team.
- Show how you work with team members to find mutually beneficial solutions to conflicts, and how you consider the needs and goals of all team members when developing potential solutions.

Question 21
How do you establish clear expectations and goals for your team?

Model Response

Establishing clear expectations and goals for my team is crucial. To approach setting expectations and goals, I focus on being clear and specific, involving team members in the process, and regularly reviewing and updating goals as needed.

To be clear and specific when setting expectations and goals for my team, I make sure to clearly communicate the specific tasks or objectives that need to be achieved and provide clear guidelines or criteria for success. This might take the form of sub-goals with clear deadlines or timeframes. This helps me to ensure that team members understand what is expected of them and are able to effectively work towards achieving our goals.

To involve team members in the process of setting expectations and goals, I make sure to seek input and feedback when developing goals and objectives. I also make sure to consider the strengths and expertise of team members when setting goals and delegate tasks and responsibilities as appropriate. By involving team members in the process, I am better able to ensure that goals are aligned with the strengths and interests of team members and that they feel a sense of ownership over the goals we set.

Additionally, by regularly reviewing and updating goals as appropriate, I'm able to make sure we're on track and making adjustments wherever necessary. This progress monitoring might involve discussions that take place at regular meetings, specific check-ins to review progress, and even soliciting input and feedback from team members.

Pro Tips

- Provide concrete examples of how you have established clear expectations and goals for a team in the past. Walk the interviewer through your process of setting, pursuing, and reviewing those goals.
- Emphasize the importance of involving team members in the collaborative process of setting expectations and goals, as well as regularly reviewing and updating goals as needed.
- Demonstrate how you are clear and specific when setting expectations and goals, and how you provide clear guidelines or criteria for success. Elaborate on how you set clear deadlines or how you use timelines for monitoring and achieving these goals.

Question 22
How do you measure the success of your team and its members?

Model Response

Measuring the success of my team and its members is an important part of any managerial position. To effectively measure success, it's beneficial to first focus on setting clear and specific performance objectives, regularly reviewing progress towards these objectives, and providing feedback and support as needed.

The process of setting clear and specific performance objectives for my team involves the alignment these objectives with the overall goals and objectives of the organization. I also think it's important to involve team members in the process of setting performance objectives where appropriate to foster buy-in and agency, and to ensure that all expectations and benchmarks for success are crystal clear.

To regularly review progress towards performance objectives, I would review the corresponding data as appropriate and would hold meetings to review progress and assess the performance of team members. By keeping a pulse on our success, I can work to ensure that we are always improving, and always rowing in the same direction.

When it comes to providing feedback and support, I would be sure to regularly communicate with team members about their progress towards performance objectives and provide constructive feedback on their performance. This is something that typically happens during annual or semi-annual review meetings, but that I believe that there are benefits to engaging in those conversations more frequently, even if they're informal in nature. I would be sure to identify any areas for improvement for individual team members and for the larger team, and would provide corresponding resources or support as needed to help everyone achieve their performance objectives.

Pro Tips

- Explain how you have measured the success of a team and its members in the past. If you can, speak to your experience using data to measure performance, as well as any experiences you might have sharing performance data with team members in a meaningful way.
- Emphasize the importance of setting clear and specific performance objectives and regularly reviewing progress towards these objectives. Be prepared to answer follow-up questions involving different scenarios, such as when a team member is highly successful versus when a team member is falling significantly short of the team's success measurement metrics.
- Show how you provide feedback and offer support as needed to help team members achieve their performance objectives, and how you identify areas for improvement and provide resources or support as needed.

Question 23
How do you handle unexpected changes or challenges that may arise within a project or team?

Model Response
Handling unexpected changes or challenges that may arise within a project or team is an inevitable part of the job, and it's part of what keeps every day interesting in this kind of leadership role. In the face of unexpected changes or challenges, I think it's most important to remain calm and composed, to identify and evaluate potential solutions, and to communicate with team members and stakeholders as needed.

Stay calm and composed when facing unexpected changes or challenges is easier said than done, but I always make sure to take a step back and take a deep breath before reacting. It's so important to keep a positive and solution-focused mindset, and to stay focused on the ultimate goals and objectives of the project or team. By staying calm and composed, I'm able to better assess the situation and develop a plan to be proactive and to move forward in the best possible way.

To identify and evaluate potential solutions to unexpected changes or challenges, I first gather all relevant information and consider the potential impacts of different options. I also make sure to involve team members and stakeholders in the process of identifying and evaluating potential solutions, and to consider the needs and goals of all parties involved. The goal is to take a proactive and strategic approach to addressing unexpected changes or challenges.

Communicating with team members and stakeholders when facing unexpected challenges is also imperative, so I make sure to keep everyone informed of any updates or changes and seek input and feedback as needed. I clearly communicate any decisions or actions taken in response, and provide any necessary support or resources to team members as needed. By communicating effectively with team members and stakeholders, I am able to maintain transparency and build trust and support as we navigate unexpected changes or challenges.

Pro Tips

- Explain how you have handled unexpected changes or challenges within a project or team in the past. Focus on how you are able to remain calm while assessing the new situation and adjusting your plans accordingly.
- Emphasize the importance of remaining calm and composed, especially in the context of stressful or unexpected situations. Elaborate on how you are able to maintain a positive and solution-focused mindset when facing unanticipated challenges.
- Describe how you communicate with team members and stakeholders as needed when facing unexpected changes or challenges, and how you keep everyone informed and seek input and feedback as needed. Demonstrate your commitment to transparency and effective communication.

Question 24
How do you foster open communication and collaboration within your team?

Model Response

To foster open communication and collaboration, I make it a point to create a safe and inclusive environment, to actively listen to and seek input from team members, and to hold meetings where everyone can meaningfully contribute.

To create a safe and inclusive environment for open communication and collaboration, I make sure to establish clear expectations for respectful and constructive communication, and to create opportunities for team members to share their ideas and perspectives. I also make sure to create a welcoming and supportive culture, and to actively encourage team members to share their thoughts and ideas. I want everyone to feel comfortable being open and honest.

As far as actively listening and seeking input from team members, I make sure to carefully pay attention to what team members are saying, to ask open-ended questions, and seek clarification as needed. I also make sure to consider the perspectives and ideas of all team members, and to provide opportunities for them to share their thoughts and ideas. By actively listening and seeking input from team members, I'm able to encourage open and honest communication and collaboration and to better understand the needs and goals of my team.

And lastly, I make sure to set up regular meetings or check-ins to discuss progress, to address any issues or challenges, and to share updates and ideas. These meetings create a great opportunity for open, honest communication, and for collaboration.

Pro Tips

- Be specific about how you have fostered open communication and collaboration within a team in the past.
- Emphasize the importance of creating a safe and inclusive environment for open communication and collaboration. You might discuss the importance of actively listening and seeking input from team members.
- Explain how you would regularly hold team meetings and check-ins to encourage open and honest communication and collaboration, and to stay connected with your team. Focus on your commitment to fostering open communication and collaboration.

Question 25

How do you ensure that team members feel heard and valued in decision-making processes?

Model Response

Ensuring that team members feel heard and valued in decision-making processes is an important part of being a leader. To ensure that team members feel heard and valued, I try to create frequent opportunities for team members to share their ideas and perspectives. I regularly seek input from all members of the team, and I make it clear how I'm considering the needs and goals of all team members when making decisions.

To create opportunities for team members to share their ideas and perspectives, I ask them to share their thoughts and ideas during meetings and to share input during decision-making processes. I encourage team members to speak up and share their perspectives, and to contribute to the overall safe and inclusive environment.

When decisions are ultimately made with team input, I make sure to articulate how the perspectives and ideas of all team members were considered and incorporated into the decision-making process. This, too, helps to reinforce the notion that every team member is valued, an important part of the organization, and critical to the decision-making process.

Pro Tips

- Be prepared to share examples that will help the interviewer get a better understanding of your approach to ensuring that team members feel heard and valued.
- Speak to the importance of creating opportunities for team members to share their ideas and

perspectives.

- Illustrate how you would consider the needs and goals of all team members when making decisions, and how you involve team members in the decision-making process as appropriate. This can help to demonstrate your commitment to ensuring that all team members truly feel heard and valued in decision-making processes.

Question 26
How would you use data in your management position?

Model Response
As a manager, I believe that data plays a crucial role in decision-making and strategic planning. In my experience, I have used data in a few different ways to drive my team's success.

I would certainly use data to track and analyze our team's performance metrics. This could includes things like productivity, customer satisfaction, and revenue. By monitoring these metrics, I can identify areas where we are excelling and areas where we need to improve. This would help me to make data-driven decisions regarding how to allocate resources and set goals for the team.

I would also use data to inform my team's strategic planning. I regularly review market research and industry trends to identify opportunities and potential threats, which would be beneficial in terms of helping us stay ahead of the curve and make informed decisions about the direction of our projects and the company as a whole.

Data is also central to communicating our team's progress and results to stakeholders. Any regular reports and dashboards that I would generate would be used to clearly and effectively communicate our key metrics and achievements. This helps us gain buy-in from stakeholders and build trust across the organization, all in a data-driven manner.

Pro Tips
- Come prepared with examples of how you have used data in the past and the impact it had on your team or organization.
- Emphasize your ability to use data to make

decisions and drive results.
- Elaborate on how you can effectively communicate data to stakeholders and upper management.

Question 27
How do you manage and track progress on multiple projects or tasks at once?

Model Response

As a manager, effectively managing and tracking progress on multiple projects or tasks at once is an important and potentially challenging part of my role. My approach involves establishing clear goals and timelines, breaking down tasks into smaller, manageable chunks, and then regularly reviewing and adjusting my approach as needed.

The first step of establishing clear goals and timelines requires me to clearly identify and communicate the overall objectives and timeframes I'm working with for each project. That puts everything into perspective, and allows me to break down those goals even further into specific tasks and milestones. Setting deadlines and expectations for the completion tasks creates accountability, whether it's to myself, to the project, to the team, or to the organization. All of this helps me to effectively manage and track progress on multiple projects and to ensure that everything that needs to get done is, indeed, getting done.

From a leadership perspective, it's also important to note that breaking down larger tasks or projects into smaller, more manageable pieces makes it possible to assign and delegate specific tasks or responsibilities to team members as appropriate. That process also requires that I make sure to prioritize tasks and responsibilities based on their importance and urgency, and to adjust my approach as needed to ensure that tasks are being completed efficiently and effectively.

Pro Tips
- Be specific about how you have effectively managed

and tracked progress on multiple projects or tasks in the past. If you can't draw from previous examples, be prepared to share a hypothetical scenario. You might discuss a framework for managing multiple projects, or even some apps and software that you believe could be beneficial.

- Emphasize the importance of establishing clear goals and timelines, and of breaking down tasks into smaller, manageable pieces.
- Explain how you believe in regularly reviewing and adjusting your approach as needed based on the needs and goals of the team.

Question 28

How do you handle team members who are not meeting their performance expectations or deadlines?

Model Response

As a manager and a leader, it is my duty to ensure that all team members are meeting their performance expectations and deadlines. When I encounter a team member who is not meeting these expectations, I first try to understand exactly what's going on so that I might get to the root cause of the issue. This would involve having a conversation with the team member to better understand their perspective and any challenges or roadblocks that they are facing.

Once I have a better understanding of the issue, I work with the team member to develop a plan to address the problem. This could be as straightforward as setting specific goals and targets for improvement, providing additional resources or support, or adjusting the team member's responsibilities or workload as needed. After that, I would make sure to regularly check in with the team member to track their progress and to provide ongoing support and guidance as needed.

In cases where the team member is not able to meet their performance expectations or deadlines despite my efforts to support and assist them, I may need to consider more formal corrective action. This might involve working with HR or upper management to develop a performance improvement plan, or potentially taking disciplinary action if the situation warrants it.

Pro Tips

- Emphasize your approach to understanding the root cause of the issue before taking any action.
- Explain how you would work with team members

to develop a plan to address performance issues and how you might provide ongoing support and guidance as needed.

- Highlight your willingness to take formal corrective action if necessary, while also emphasizing your commitment to helping team members succeed and improve their performance.

Question 29
How do you build trust and credibility with your team?

Model Response
Trust and credibility is foundational for so much of what we do, and it's an absolutely essential part of being a manager. To build trust and credibility with my team, I make a point of being transparent and open with my communication, being reliable and consistent in my actions, and being a supportive and approachable leader.

To be transparent and open with my communication, I make sure to clearly communicate my expectations, goals, and plans with my team, and to be open to feedback and suggestions. I also make sure to be transparent about any challenges or issues that may arise, and to provide regular updates and progress reports to my team. Trust often breaks down when members of the team feel like they are being lied to or purposefully kept in the dark, and credibility erodes anytime anyone intentionally skirts the truth. So, in short, it's my goal to avoid both of those things by being transparent and open with my communication, and by consistently demonstrating my willingness to be open and honest.

Being reliable and consistent requires that I follow through on my commitments and that I'm predictable, in a good way, when it comes to my approach to leading and managing my team. I also make sure to be responsive and accessible to my team to the greatest extent possible so that I can address their concerns and questions as they arise. All of these things are interwoven: trust, credibility, dependability, honesty, and approachability.

Pro Tips
* Elaborate on how you make it a point to be

transparent and open in your communication, and how that helps to build trust and credibility with your team.

- Explain how you are reliable and consistent in your actions. Be prepared to concretely describe what this looks like, as well as how it contributes to trust and credibility.
- Highlight your approach to being a supportive and approachable leader. Consider offering points of contrast, such explaining what could go wrong in scenarios where a leader is not approachable, credible, or trustworthy, to illustrate your understanding of why this is a critical facet the job.

Question 30
How do you handle difficult or sensitive conversations with team members, such as addressing performance issues or conflicts?

Model Response
As a manager, handling difficult or sensitive conversations with team members is an important part of my role. To handle these types of conversations effectively, I focus on being clear and direct in my communication, being respectful and empathetic towards the team member, and being solution-oriented in my approach.

At the onset of the conversation, I make sure to clearly articulate the issue or concern that needs to be addressed, and to provide specific examples or evidence to support my position. I also make it a point to listen actively and to seek to understand the team member's perspective. By being clear and direct in my communication, I am able to effectively convey my concerns and to address the issue in a straightforward manner.

It's also incredibly important to be respectful and empathetic towards the team member, especially in the context of handling a difficult of sensitive conversation, so I make sure to approach the conversation with a non-judgmental attitude and to show understanding and compassion towards their perspective. Framing the problem as something that isn't personal, but a matter of running an effective organization, can help to foster a meaningful and respectful dialogue, too. I also make sure to acknowledge any valid points that the team member may share during the conversation, and generally avoid placing blame or assigning fault unless that is inherent to the discussion. Being respectful and empathetic towards the team member can go a long way as far as maintaining a positive and supportive environment for the conversation.

And finally, I would be as solution-oriented as possible in my approach. That means that I would focus on finding ways to address the issue and to move forward. This might involve developing a plan of action to address the issue, providing additional resources or support, or adjusting the team member's responsibilities or workload as needed. In the end, this conversation could strengthen our relationship, and would invariably strengthen our team.

Pro Tips

- Emphasize your approach to clear and direct communication and how it helps to effectively address difficult or sensitive issues.
- Show how you are respectful and empathetic towards team members and how this helps to create a positive and supportive environment for difficult or sensitive conversations.
- Highlight your approach to being solution-oriented and how it helps to find ways to address difficult or sensitive issues and move forward.

Question 31
How do you approach team building and team bonding activities?

Model Response

Building strong and cohesive teams is essential for achieving success, and team building or team bonding activities can be an effective way to do that — but I think it's important to take a strategic and thoughtful approach.

First, I like to make sure to clearly communicate the goals and objectives of these activities, and to ensure that they align with the overall goals and objectives of the team. This can be helpful as far as letting everyone know that we are invested in developing a cohesive team culture, and can make some of the otherwise hokey facets of team building feel like they are serving a more meaningful objective. I also make sure to consider the interests and preferences of my team members and to select activities that are engaging and enjoyable for everyone.

Next, I it's important to facilitate these activities in a way that promotes active participation and teamwork. This may involve setting clear roles and responsibilities for team members, providing opportunities for collaboration and problem-solving, and encouraging open communication and trust.

And finally, it's important to follow up on these activities and to reflect on their impact on team dynamics and performance. This would involve soliciting feedback from team members, analyzing data and metrics, and making adjustments as needed. What better way to learn whether the team building activities were effective, and whether they should be implemented again in the same manner?

Pro Tips

- Emphasize the importance of aligning team building activities with the overall goals and objectives of the team and the organization.
- Discuss how you consider the interests and preferences of team members so as to ensure that team building activities don't inadvertently have the opposite effect. Explain how you would go about choosing activities that are engaging and enjoyable for everyone.
- Highlight your approach to facilitating these activities in a way that promotes active participation and teamwork, and how you follow up on and reflect on their impact on team dynamics and performance.

Question 32
How do you handle conflicting priorities or demands from different stakeholders?

Model Response
As a manager, I understand that conflicting priorities or demands from different stakeholders are a common challenge that must be effectively managed. When faced with these situations, my approach is to prioritize and triage the demands, considering their relative importance and urgency, and to communicate openly and transparently with all stakeholders.

I would begin by taking the time to fully understand the needs and priorities of each stakeholder and to clearly communicate my own priorities and objectives. This helps to ensure that there is a shared understanding of the situation and that all parties are working towards common goals.

I work also work to identify any areas of overlap or synergy between the demands of different stakeholders and to find ways to address these in a mutually beneficial way. This may involve seeking input or feedback from stakeholders, identifying areas of compromise, or finding creative solutions that meet the needs of all parties involved.

I would make sure to continuously reassess and adjust my priorities as needed, in light of changing circumstances or new information. This helps to ensure that my team and I are able to effectively respond to changing demands and to stay aligned with the overall goals and objectives of the organization.

Pro Tips
- Emphasize the importance of fully understanding the needs and priorities of all stakeholders and communicating your own priorities clearly.

- Discuss how you identify areas of overlap or synergy between conflicting demands and work to find mutually beneficial solutions.
- Highlight your approach to continuously reassessing and adjusting your priorities in light of changing circumstances or new information.

Question 33
How do you approach setting and achieving diversity and inclusion goals for your team?

Model Response

I understand that diversity and inclusion are key to building strong, effective teams and organizations. When it comes to setting and achieving diversity and inclusion goals, my approach is centered on building a culture of respect and inclusivity, and on actively seeking out and valuing diverse perspectives and experiences.

First and foremost, I work to establish clear diversity and inclusion goals and objectives for my team, and to communicate these clearly to all team members. This helps to ensure that everyone is working towards a common vision and that all team members feel valued and included.

I also work to create a culture that is welcoming and inclusive to people of all backgrounds and experiences. This could involve implementing diversity and inclusion training or initiatives, fostering open and respectful communication, and creating opportunities for team members to come together and build relationships.

And finally, I make sure to actively seek out and value diverse perspectives and experiences within my team. This might involve seeking out diverse candidates for open positions, encouraging open and respectful dialogue within the team, and actively seeking out and incorporating diverse perspectives in decision-making processes.

Pro Tips
- Emphasize the importance of setting clear diversity and inclusion goals and objectives, and of

communicating these goals to all team members.
- Discuss your approach to building a culture that is welcoming and inclusive to people of all backgrounds and experiences.
- Highlight your commitment to actively seeking out and valuing diverse perspectives and experiences within your team.

Question 34
How do you handle and support team members who are experiencing personal or professional challenges?

Model Response
I understand that team members may face personal or professional challenges that can impact their work and well-being. When it comes to handling and supporting team members in these situations, my approach is centered on empathy, understanding, and creating a supportive environment.

I make sure to listen to team members and understand their needs and concerns. This is all about having open and honest conversations about their challenges and the support they need to overcome them.

I would also work to create a supportive environment that promotes well-being and resilience. This could involve implementing initiatives to support the mental health and well-being of the entire team or organization. With this kind of larger architecture in place, it would be even easier to offer resources and support to help specific team members through difficult times.

I also make sure to be available and approachable as a manager. I'm always willing to offer support and guidance as needed, and I understand that team members may need extra support or accommodations during challenging times.

Pro Tips
- Emphasize the importance of listening to and understanding team members' needs and concerns.
- Discuss your approach to creating a supportive environment that promotes well-being and resilience.

- Highlight your commitment to being available and approachable as a manager and to offering support and guidance as needed.

Question 35
How do you approach training and onboarding new team members?

Model Response

I believe it is important to set clear expectations and goals for new team members from the start. This includes providing them with a thorough overview of their responsibilities and the expectations for their performance, as well as setting specific goals for their development and growth within the team.

To support new team members in their onboarding process, I make sure to provide them with all of the necessary resources and tools they need to succeed. This might include access to training materials, one-on-one mentorship, and opportunities to shadow more experienced team members. I also make myself available for any questions or concerns they may have as they get up to speed.

In terms of training, I believe in a hands-on approach. I prefer to give new team members the opportunity to learn by doing, rather than simply providing them with information. This might include assigning them tasks or projects that are tailored to their skill level and providing them with guidance and support as they work through them.

Pro Tips

- Be prepared to share specific examples of how you have successfully onboarded and trained new team members in the past.
- Emphasize the importance of setting clear expectations and providing the necessary resources and support to help new team members succeed.
- Consider highlighting any innovative or creative approaches you have taken to training and

onboarding in the past.

CURVEBALLS

Question 36
What do you consider to be your biggest weakness as a leader?

Model Response

As a leader, one of my biggest weaknesses is taking on too many tasks and projects. In the past, this has stretched me thin in terms of managing my time effectively and created unnecessary stress. I was able to keep up the quality of my work, but taking on too many projects and tasks is unsustainable for anyone.

To address this weakness, I have implemented a number of strategies, including creating more detailed and realistic to-do lists, delegating tasks to team members when appropriate, and setting boundaries around my availability. I have also sought out resources such as time management workshops and productivity apps to help me better manage my workload.

Pro Tips

- Be honest and authentic in your response. Admitting to a weakness shows vulnerability and humility, which are important qualities in a leader. That said, consider sharing a weakness that can also be represented as a strength, rather than a weakness that might be interpreted as solely a liability.
- Provide specific examples and details to illustrate your weakness and how you are working to address it. This shows self-awareness and a proactive approach to improvement.
- Emphasize the steps you are taking to overcome your weakness and improve as a leader. This demonstrates your commitment to personal and

professional growth.

Question 37
How do you handle criticism or negative feedback from team members or stakeholders?

Model Response

It's important to be open to constructive criticism and feedback in order to continuously improve and grow, especially in a leadership role. When I receive negative feedback, I try to approach it with a growth mindset and see it as an opportunity to learn and develop.

One approach that has worked well for me in the past is to first thank the person for their feedback and actively listen to what they have to say. I try to understand their perspective and the reasoning behind their criticism. I also ask clarifying questions to ensure that I fully understand their concerns.

Once I have a good understanding of the feedback, I reflect on it and consider whether it is valid and how it aligns with my own goals and values as a leader. If I agree with the feedback, I work on a plan to address it and improve in that area. If I disagree, I try to have a respectful and open dialogue about our different perspectives and see if there is a way to find common ground or a compromise.

Pro Tips

- Describe how you would practice active listening and show that you value the feedback you are receiving by thanking the person and asking clarifying questions.
- Demonstrate that you approach criticism with a growth mindset and see it as an opportunity to learn and develop.
- Explain that you would have a plan in place for

addressing valid feedback and be open to having a respectful dialogue about any disagreement.

Question 38
Have you ever had to make a difficult decision that was not popular with your team?

Model Response

One difficult decision that I had to make as a leader was when I had to let go of a team member who was not meeting performance expectations. It was a difficult decision because the team member was a long-time employee and well-liked by the team, but their performance had consistently been below par and had not improved despite multiple coaching and development efforts.

I approached the situation with transparency and honesty, explaining to the team member the specific areas where their performance was lacking and the impact it was having on the team and the organization. I also offered support and resources to help them improve, but ultimately, it became clear that the best course of action for the team and the organization was to part ways.

This decision was not popular with the team, as they had strong personal connections with the team member and were sad to see them go. However, I made it clear that the decision was not made lightly and was in the best interests of the team and the organization. In the end, the team was able to move forward and continue to be successful, and I believe that my approach to the situation helped to maintain trust and respect within the team.

Pro Tips

- Be honest and transparent in your response. It's important to be upfront about the situation and your thought process in making the decision.
- Emphasize the importance of the team and the organization in your decision-making process. This

shows that you prioritize the success of the team and the organization above personal relationships.

- Show how you took steps to support and help the team member before making the decision to let them go. This can demonstrate your commitment to development and growth for all team members.

Question 39
Have you ever had to make a tough call on a project that went against your personal values or beliefs?

Model Response
When I was leading a team at my previous company, I was faced with a situation where we were asked to work on a project for a client that was known for their unethical business practices. I knew that taking on this project would go against my personal values and beliefs, and I also knew that it could potentially damage the reputation of our company.

After careful consideration, I decided to decline the project and explain my reasoning to the client. This was a difficult decision because it meant potentially losing a lucrative opportunity, but I felt that it was important to stand by my values and not compromise on what I believed was right.

In the end, the client respected my decision and we were able to find alternative opportunities that aligned with our values. I learned that it is important to be transparent and authentic as a leader, and to always consider the long-term impact of my decisions.

Pro Tips
- Be prepared to talk about a difficult decision you've made as a leader, and explain how you approached the situation and what you learned from it. You may be asked to share more specific details about the situation, so be prepared to provide them in a concrete way.
- Emphasize your personal values and beliefs, and how you apply them in your leadership style.
- Practice giving thoughtful and well-reasoned

response to question that places you in an ethical dilemma such as this one. There isn't necessary a right or wrong answer, but rather, an opportunity for you to showcase your values and beliefs and to learn whether they are congruent with those of the organization where you are interviewing.

Question 40
How do you handle working under tight deadlines or high pressure situations?

Model Response

As a manager, I understand that tight deadlines and high pressure situations are a normal part of the job. To handle these situations, I try to remain calm and focused, and I prioritize tasks to ensure that the most important ones are completed first. I've learned that the more of those high pressure situations we face, the easier it is to remain calm in those contexts. I also prioritize communicating clearly with my team and relevant stakeholders, setting realistic expectations and regularly updating them on the progress of the project. Many individuals avoid that kind of communication in high pressure situations, but I believe it's even more important when tensions are high and deadlines are close.

Beyond those high pressure situations, I think it's important to take breaks and prioritize self-care where appropriate. This helps me to stay productive and on top of my game, and I encourage my team to engage in similar practices in order to maintain a healthy work-life balance and to avoid burnout. Appropriate self-care can make us even more efficient and effective when the going gets tough.

Pro Tips
- Prepare for this kind of question by thinking about examples of times when you have worked under tight deadlines or high pressure situations and how you approached them. Emphasize your ability to stay calm and focused in stressful situations.
- Consider discussing specific strategies you use to

break down large projects into smaller tasks and delegate responsibilities to team members.

- Mention any techniques you use to stay calm and manage stress, such as taking breaks or practicing deep breathing.

Question 41
Have you ever had to let go of a team member for performance reasons?

Model Response

There have been a few instances where I have had to let go of a team member for performance reasons. It is never an easy decision, as I understand that people's careers and livelihoods are at stake. However, as a leader, it is my responsibility to ensure that the team is performing at its best and meeting the goals and objectives of the organization.

When faced with the situation of having to let go of a team member, I approach it with empathy and professionalism. I make sure to have an open and honest conversation with the individual about their performance and provide them with clear and specific feedback about areas for improvement. I also offer resources and support to help them improve, such as additional training or mentorship.

If, after these efforts, the team member's performance does not improve to the level that is necessary for the success of the team and the organization, I make the difficult decision to let them go. Depending on the organization and established practices, this is likely to be a decision made collaboratively with other managers, or with upper-management. Ultimately, I approach the overall process this with respect and sensitivity, ensuring that the team member is treated fairly and given the opportunity to ask questions or provide feedback.

Pro Tips
- Be honest and transparent about your experiences. If you have had to let go of a team member for performance reasons, it is better to be upfront about

it rather than trying to hide it.

- Emphasize the steps you would have taken to try to improve the team member's performance before letting them go. Use this as an opportunity to show that you are proactive and willing to put in effort to help your team succeed.

- Explain how you would demonstrate empathy and professionalism when discussing the situation. It is important to show that you understand the impact your actions have on others and that you handle difficult situations with grace and respect.

Question 42
How do you balance being a team player with being a leader?

Model Response

It is important, and potentially challenging, to strike a balance between being a team player and being a leader. On one hand, it is important to actively participate in team efforts and contribute to the team's success. This can involve collaborating with team members, offering support and resources, and being willing to roll up my sleeves and do the work alongside my team. At the same time, it is also important to lead and guide the team towards achieving our goals and objectives. This involves setting clear expectations, providing direction and support, and making tough decisions when necessary. When these roles are out of balance, it can lead to problematic leadership, to burn-out, or to all sorts of other problematic scenarios.

So, to balance these two roles, I focus on being transparent and open with my team. I communicate my expectations and goals clearly and openly, and I am always willing to listen to the perspectives and ideas of my team members. I also make a conscious effort to involve my team in decision-making processes and to seek out their input and feedback, but also strive to delegate responsibilities wherever appropriate so that I can effectively focus on managerial responsibilities and leadership tasks. This helps to create a sense of ownership and buy-in among the team, and allows me to effectively lead and guide the team towards success.

Pro Tips

- Be authentic and genuine about your leadership style. Use this as an opportunity to share your values and beliefs, and your willingness to be open and transparent with your team.

- Emphasize that you prioritize communicating openly. Explain that clear and open communication is key to building trust and credibility with your team, and elaborate on how you would make a conscious effort to keep your team informed and involved in decision-making processes.
- Explain how you would regularly seek out feedback to ensure that you are balancing these two roles. Regularly soliciting feedback from your team can help you to better understand their needs and concerns, and can help you to adjust your leadership style accordingly.

Question 43
How do you handle a team member who consistently challenges your authority or decisions?

Model Response
It's important to approach situations like these with a level head and an open mind. My first step would be to have a one-on-one conversation with the team member to understand their perspective and any underlying concerns they may have. It's possible that they may have valid points or ideas that could contribute to the success of the team. I would also let the individual know that it's okay to contribute meaningfully to team discussions and collaborative decision-making opportunities, but in the end, we must work together as a cohesive team. Challenging my authority or undermining my decisions is not an appropriate or acceptable course of action.

Hopefully, those conversations would redirect that team member's behavior moving forward. But if the challenges to my authority or decisions continue to disrupt the team's productivity and morale, I would need to take more decisive action. This could involve setting clearer and more formal boundaries and expectations, seeking support from upper management, or, in extreme cases, considering whether the team member's continued presence on the team is in the best interest of the group.

Pro Tips
- Explain how you would stay calm and try to understand the other person's perspective before reacting.
- Describe how you would set clear expectations and boundaries for team members, and communicate

them clearly.

- Don't be afraid to seek support from upper management or HR if needed, but be sure to clarify that this would not be the first step you would take in the face of a challenging situation.

Question 44
Have you ever had to pivot or change course on a project due to unexpected challenges or changes?

Model Response

Change is a constant part of the work environment and it's important to be agile and adaptable. One situation that comes to mind is when I was managing a project for a new product launch. We had a tight deadline and were making good progress, but halfway through the project we received feedback from market research that the target audience preferred a different design. Rather than pushing forward with the original plan, I made the decision to pivot and rework the design to align with the new information. It was a tough call, as it meant going back to the drawing board and potentially delaying the launch, but ultimately it was the right decision for the success of the product.

To pivot effectively, I made sure to communicate the change in direction clearly to the team and provide them with the resources and support they needed to adjust to the new plan. I also made sure to keep stakeholders informed and on board with the changes. In the end, the revised product was well received by the target audience and we were able to meet the deadline thanks to the team's hard work and flexibility. It wasn't the easier choice, but it was the right choice and, in my opinion, the choice that had to be made.

Pro Tips

- Be honest and transparent about any challenges or changes you faced on a project. Don't try to sugarcoat or downplay the challenge, as it shows that you are capable of handling tough situations and making tough decisions.

- Emphasize your ability to adapt and pivot as needed. Demonstrate that you are flexible and can think on your feet.
- Highlight any positive outcomes that came from the change or pivot. Use this as an opportunity to show that you are able to turn challenges into opportunities and drive success for the team and the organization.

Question 45
Where do you see yourself in five years?

Model Response

As a managerial leader, it is important to have a vision for the future and a clear direction for where I see myself and my team heading. In five years, I see myself continuing to grow and develop as a leader, building upon the skills and experiences I have gained thus far. I also hope to be leading a team that is not only successful in achieving its goals, but is also a cohesive and supportive group that values diversity, inclusivity, and open communication. In other words, I want to keep doing what I'm doing, and I want to be even better at it.

In terms of specific career aspirations, I'm committed to staying up-to-date on industry trends and constantly seeking out new opportunities for learning and growth. I'm driven by a desire to make a positive impact and contribute to the success of the organization I am a part of. In five years, I'd be happy to have progressed to a higher leadership role with even more responsibility and influence within the company.

Pro Tips
- Be honest and authentic. It's okay if you don't have a specific five-year plan mapped out, but be genuine in your response and share your values and long-term goals.
- Emphasize your commitment to growth and development. Show that you are dedicated to constantly learning and improving, and that you are open to new challenges and opportunities.
- Highlight your vision for the future of the organization. Share your ideas and goals for how

you can contribute to the success of the company in the long term. Likewise, avoid sharing a five-year plan that entails leaving the company before you've even joined it.

SCENARIOS

Question 46

Your team has been working on a high-stakes project for the past six months. The deadline is fast approaching and your team has made significant progress, but there are still a few key tasks that need to be completed before the project can be considered a success. One of your team members, Jane, has consistently been falling behind on her tasks and has not been meeting her deadlines. You have tried to provide additional support and resources, but Jane's performance has not improved. You have also noticed that Jane has been consistently coming in late to work and has been taking longer breaks than usual. You have a meeting with the project sponsor in two days and you are concerned about Jane's ability to meet the remaining deadlines and contribute to the success of the project. How do you address the situation with Jane and ensure that the project is completed on time and to the best of your team's ability?

Model Response

First, I would try to understand the root cause of Jane's performance issues. This would include talking to Jane privately to see if there are any personal or professional challenges that might be impacting her work, and it would also involve seeking feedback from other team members to see if there are any areas where I might provide additional support or resources.

Assuming that Jane's performance issues are not related to any extraneous personal or professional challenges, the next step would be to set clear expectations and goals for Jane's remaining tasks and deadlines. This would involve setting specific, measurable, achievable, relevant, and time-bound (SMART) goals for Jane, as well as establishing a clear plan for how she can meet these goals. This would work to give Jane a clear roadmap for moving forward in an acceptable way, while providing me with a tangible means of monitoring Jane's progress.

In addition to setting clearer expectations and goals, I would also work with Jane to identify any roadblocks or challenges that might be preventing her from meeting her deadlines. This could include providing additional training or resources, or finding ways to streamline processes or eliminate unnecessary tasks. Jane might not even be aware of the roadblocks, so observing her workflow could help me to troubleshoot the issue, too.

If, after taking these steps, Jane's performance does not improve, I would consider other options, such as reassigning tasks to other team members, picking up the necessary slack myself, or seeking additional support from other departments and external resources. Of course, this would also be documented in Jane's file and could impact her future on the team, but ultimately, my goal would be to find a solution that allows the project to be completed on time and to the best of our ability, while also being fair and respectful to Jane as a team member.

Pro Tips

- Explain how you would focus on understanding the root cause of the issue before jumping to any conclusions or taking action. This could involve seeking feedback from other team members or looking for underlying personal or professional challenges that might be impacting the individual's performance.
- Discuss how you might help rectify the performance issues, such as by setting clearer expectations and tangible goals for the individual. Using SMART goal setting principles can be a helpful way to

accomplish this by ensuring that the individual knows exactly what is expected of them and has a clear plan for how to meet these expectations.

- Reflect on the situation and consider any potential consequences or impacts of my decision on the team, the project, and the organization as a whole. This could include financial implications, effects on team morale or productivity, or potential impacts on the organization's reputation or stakeholders.

Question 47

Your team has been working on a project for several months, and it's approaching its deadline. However, you've just received new information that one of the key assumptions you made at the beginning of the project was incorrect. This information could potentially impact the entire project and potentially lead to failure. How do you approach this situation and what steps do you take to address the potential impact on the project?

Model Response

If I were faced with this situation, my first step would be to assess the scope and impact of the incorrect assumption on the project. I would gather as much information as possible about the situation and consult with my team to understand the full extent of the potential impact.

Once I have a clear understanding of the situation, I would immediately notify any stakeholders or superiors about the potential impact on the project. It's important to be transparent and upfront about any issues that may arise, as this helps to mitigate potential damage and allows for a more effective solution to be developed. If the source of this issue was a decision or assumption made on my part, I would not shy away from owning up to it — knowing that any decisions or assumptions that I make are always guided by the information we have at hand. Being a leader means owning up to the choices that we make, but more important is working to develop a plan to address that misstep.

To that end, I would work with my team to develop a plan to address the incorrect assumption and its potential impact on the project. This might involve revising our approach or strategy, reallocating resources, or seeking additional support. It's important to involve the entire team in this process, as everyone has valuable insights and perspectives that can help to find a solution.

Once the project is back on course, I would seek to learn what caused the initial incorrect assumption so that we, as a team, can learn from our mistakes and be sure not to make the same error again in the future. This might be the most important step in the entire sequence of events I've just described. Ultimately, my primary goal would be to minimize the impact of the incorrect assumption on the project and its deadline as much as possible, and immediately after that, my goal would be to ensure the problem does not repeat itself.

Pro Tips

- Be transparent and upfront about any issues or challenges that may arise. Do not shy away from owning up to an assumption, choice, or decision that you made at the onset of the project, but be proactive and seek to learn from this experience.
- Involve the entire team in finding a solution to the problem.
- Stay focused and committed to finding a solution, even in the face of challenges or setbacks.

Question 48

Your team is working on a project that involves collaborating with another team from a different department. The other team is known for being difficult to work with and frequently causing delays and issues with projects. You have noticed that your team is starting to become frustrated and demotivated due to the constant challenges and roadblocks that the other team is causing. How do you handle the situation and work with the other team to ensure that the project is successful, while also maintaining the motivation and morale of your team?

Model Response

In this situation, it is important to first assess the root cause of the issues with the other team. Are they lacking necessary resources or support? Is there a misalignment of goals or expectations? Once the underlying cause has been identified, I would approach the situation in a few steps:

I would communicate openly and transparently with both teams. It is important to be honest about the challenges that are being faced and the impact they are having on the project. This will help to establish trust and open up the possibility for finding a solution together.

I would also work with the other team to establish clear goals and expectations. By setting specific and measurable targets, it will be easier to track progress and identify areas of improvement.

I would implement a process for regular check-ins and progress updates. This will help to ensure that both teams are aligned and can address any issues or roadblocks in a timely manner. I would also seek to foster open communication and collaboration between the teams, and would encourage team members to share their ideas and provide feedback in a constructive manner. This would help to build a positive working relationship and create a more collaborative environment.

If the other team had a team leader or manager, I would make it a point to articulate this issue with them, and to work with them on all of the steps I just mentioned. That would ensure a cohesive and unified approach to help our teams work together in a meaningful way that maintains the motivation and morale for all parties involved. We could provide additional support or resources, highlight recognize contributions across both teams, and find additional ways to make the work more enjoyable.

Pro Tips

- Explain the ways in which you would practice active listening and effective communication skills. Elaborate on how these would be key in working with a difficult team and finding a solution to the challenges being faced.
- Describe how you would be proactive in addressing potential issues and roadblocks. Explain how you would not wait for problems to arise before taking action, but rather, would be proactive in finding solutions and preventing them from happening in the first place.
- Clarify how you would stay positive and focused on the ultimate goal. It can be easy to get discouraged when working with a difficult team, but it's important to stay motivated and keep the end result in mind.

Question 49

You have been managing a team for several years and have developed strong relationships with each team member. However, your company is going through a restructuring and you have been asked to take on a new team with a completely different group of people. Many of the new team members have been with the company for a shorter period of time and are at a lower level in the organization. How do you approach building relationships and trust with the new team, while also maintaining your credibility and leadership as the manager?

Model Response

As a manager, it's important to approach situations like this with empathy and understanding. I would start by taking the time to get to know each team member individually and understand their strengths, goals, and any challenges they may be facing. Building trust and relationships is a two-way street, so it would be important to be transparent and open with the team about my own goals and expectations as well.

I would also make an effort to create a positive and inclusive work environment, where team members feel comfortable voicing their opinions and ideas. This includes actively listening to their feedback and concerns, and being open to hearing different perspectives.

In terms of maintaining credibility and leadership, I would focus on being consistent and fair in my decision-making and communication with the team. The same principles that brought me success with my previous team would likely hold true with this new team, too. This would also include staying up-to-date on industry trends and best practices, being open to learning from the team and seeking out new opportunities for growth and development, and growing together as a cohesive team.

Pro Tips

- Describe how you would take the time to get to know each team member individually. Elaborate on how building relationships and trust is a key aspect of effective leadership, and how it starts with understanding who your team members are and what motivates them.

- Explain how you would be transparent and open with your team. Discuss how sharing your goals and expectations with the team would help to build trust and foster a sense of collaboration.

- Clarify how you would stay consistent and fair in your decision-making and communication. Speak to how this would help to maintain your credibility and leadership within the team, and could help to build trust and respect.

Question 50

Your team is working on a project that involves partnering with a vendor that has a history of unethical practices. You have received information from a reliable source that the vendor is currently engaging in deceptive and fraudulent behavior. However, the vendor is the only option for the project, and the project has a tight deadline and budget. How do you approach this ethical dilemma and what steps do you take to ensure that the project is completed successfully while also maintaining the integrity and values of your company?

Model Response

As a manager, it is my responsibility to ensure that the projects my team works on align with the values and ethics of the company. In this situation, I would first verify the information about the vendor's unethical practices with additional sources to ensure that it is accurate and reliable. If the information is confirmed, I would bring this to the attention of my superiors and recommend that we terminate our partnership with the vendor. While it may be challenging to find a new vendor in the short time frame and within the budget constraints, it is important that we prioritize ethical behavior and not compromise our values for the sake of meeting a deadline.

If, for some reason, the decision is made to continue working with the vendor, I would make sure to set clear expectations and guidelines for our interactions with them. This could include making it clear that any fraudulent or deceptive behavior will not be tolerated, and establishing clear consequences for any violations. I would also consider implementing additional checks and balances, such as having a third party review any documents or agreements with the vendor.

Pro Tips

- In general, when faced with ethical dilemmas, it is important to remember that the long-term reputation and credibility of the company are more important than short-term gains.
- It is also crucial to communicate transparently and openly with superiors and stakeholders about the situation, and to involve them in decision-making processes.
- It may be helpful to mention the possibility of seeking the advice of a mentor, the company's attorney, or an ethics committee within the company.